Apple Watch Guide

Ultimate Guide *on how to setup and master your device*

Melissa L. Moody

Table of Contents

INTRODUCTION

Did you just purchase the Apple watch and need to learn more about the device? Or have you been searching for some tips, tricks and hidden features to enable you master and push your Apple Watch to its limit? Then this book is for you.

Congratulations on acquiring the latest edition of the Apple watch family, you are well on your way to achieving more creativity and productivity. Whether you have had a previous Apple Watch series, a senior or a new User, this guide has been written with the goal of equipping you with the right information to optimize performance on your Apple Watch

CHAPTER 1

How to Use Your Apple Watch

The Apple Watch can be considered a great friend on your wrist, but it may also be somewhat intimidating. Before you figure out how to run with the Apple Watch, it is critical to check out the basics about how to use the Apple Watch to ensure you are getting all the huge benefits.

Among the countless great benefits of Apple Watch is the capability to place and get phone calls, texts and old-school email messages, rendering it a gateway to your communication. But Apple Watch is a lot more. It is an exercise device, a very good music player, a calendar, a good home controller and (of course) a fairly good time-keeper combined with the great many other things it can do.

So How Exactly Does Apple Watch Work?

When you initially take the Apple Look out of the box, you utilize the Watch application on your iPhone to create it up. Apple Watch runs on the mixture of Bluetooth and Wi-Fi to talk to the iPhone. Even though a few of its features can be utilized with no iPhone close by, other features require that link with the iPhone.

Most applications and top features of the Apple Watch require some form of data connection. You will not have the ability to place calls, text message friends, pay attention to the air or use Siri without that connection. The latest Apple Watch has a model that facilitates connecting to mobile data with no need for an iPhone, but also for the majority of us, we'll either need our iPhone close by or we should hook up to a Wi-Fi network.

How to Use Your Apple Watch's Hardware

Contrary to popular belief, some people don't even realize there's a button just underneath the digital crown for times or even weeks after buying an Apple Watch, which explains why we begins this Apple Watch tutorial with the hardware.

- **Digital crown.** The digital crown doesn't simply take us from the watch face display to the house display screen with the apps. You can even transform it to focus in and from the app display, and if you come with an app open, it'll scroll up or down within the app.

- **Side buttons.** You can dismiss the medial side button, but it is the key to three important features. First, clicking on it will open up a summary of your lately used apps, making switching backwards and forwards between applications easier. Second, keeping it down will open up the energy Off and Emergency SOS display screen. And third, carrying on to carry it down will automatically turn off these devices if for reasons unknown you are unable to get the energy Off screen to show. Like a reward, holding down both part button and the digital crown will snap a screenshot of the Apple Watch's screen.

- **Pressure Touch.** This feature is triggered by first putting a finger gently on the display and then pressing down against the screen. If performed on the watch face display screen, Push Touch will help you to customize the various watch faces. Around the app screen, it'll enable you to change to a list-oriented display rather than grid. Individual applications could also have special Power Touch functionality. For instance, using Drive Touch in the experience app will help you to see every week overview or change your move goal.

A Guide on Apple Watch Gestures

Furthermore, to hardware settings, there are many basic gestures that will really help you utilize Apple Watch to its fullest, including a concealed control panel that will help you do things such as find a lost iPhone. These gestures are similar in character to the gestures on the iPhone and iPad.

Drag and faucet. Both of these gestures define how to use the Apple Watch and can be exhibited on the application screen. Putting your finger on the screen and 'dragging' it round the screen may cause the round grid of applications to go alongside your finger. Tapping a person application with a finger will release that app.

Swipe down. The swipe gestures operate in a different

way depending on if you're on the Apple Watch's watch face. Within the watch face, a swipe down gesture, which is conducted by putting a finger on the center of the display screen and then moving it down without lifting it from the screen, starts the notification middle. This notification middle will show any texts or notifications delivered to the Apple Watch. Swiping down in an application will generally scroll up a list or web page.

Swipe up. For the watch face display, a swipe up will reveal the concealed control panel. This panel consists of shortcuts to configurations and features. Of special notice is the button with a telephone with semi-circles to either aspect. This shortcut may cause your iPhone to produce a beeping or pinging audio, which can only help you locate it behind that cushion or between your sofa cushions. Swiping up in an app will help you to scroll down a list or web page. (Keep in mind, this may also be achieved by turning the digital crown.)

Swipe remaining or right. In the watch face display screen, swiping from still left to directly on the screen changes out the watch face. You are able to swipe from right-to-left to return to an earlier watch face, or use Pressure Touch to customize the watch encounters. Swiping remaining or right in an application will have specific features with respect to the app. For instance, swiping from to left on the notification in the notification middle will help you to delete the notification or customize that kind of notification.

Zoom tap. You are able to move into or focus from the screen by double-tapping the display with two fingertips. The double touch must be performed rapidly. While zoomed into the screen, you can maneuver around the display screen by putting two fingertips on the screen and dragging them without raising them from the display.

How To Place Phone Calls, Respond To Texts And Read Email

The very best part about the Apple Watch is merely how easy it is to do the items you anticipate it to do. Apple Watch includes a lift-to-activate gesture, so simply turning and raising your wrist will activate it. This helps it be easy to simply accept a call or read a text.

Phone calls. You are able to place a telephone call the same manner you'll do etc your iPhone. Simply touch the telephone app, scroll down your connections or favorites list and touch who you want to call. Keep in mind, unless you come with an Apple Watch with a mobile connection, you'll need to be within selection of your iPhone to put the call.

Texts. Composing a text is really as easy as making a telephone call. You can even answer a text by tapping it and selecting reply. The button with a microphone will help you to use Siri to dictate an answer, as the button with a hand introduces Scribble, an insight that becomes your handwriting into text message. You should use this to pull one letter at the same time. In addition, it accepts most punctuation.

Email. Don't be concerned, there are no special hoops to leap to get email ready to go on your watch. Your email configurations are mirrored from your iPhone by default; therefore, you will get access to all your email with the same notification configurations. You can change notifications for specific inboxes on or off by starting the Watch application on your iPhone, choosing Email and then selecting Custom under Reflection my iPhone. You are able to reply to specific electronic mails by using either Siri's tone of voice dictation or the Scribble insight.

Walkie-Talkie. Another fun way to talk to the Apple Watch has been the Walkie-Talkie app. This application gives you to enter walkie-talkie setting with some other Apple Watch consumer in the world. Which is as easy to use as the telephone app. Simply touch the Walkie-Talkie icon, which is yellowish with a walkie-talkie onto it, and then choose a person from the contact list.

How to Use Siri on the Apple Watch

If you believe Siri is effective on your iPhone or iPad, it is double etc. the Apple Watch. You ought to be in a position to activate Siri simply by increasing the watch to the mouth area and providing her a control or requesting her a question. You can even use the "Hey Siri" term accompanied by your instructions.

Siri not answering? Release the Settings application on your Apple Watch, choose General and then choose Siri. You are able to toggle both Hey Siri and Increase to Speak from within the Siri configurations. For Increase to Speak, you might have the best results by speaking straight into the watch. You can even simply keep down the digital crown to talk about Siri.

Just what exactly can we do with Siri on Apple Watch?:

- "Hey Siri, what's the elements like?"

- "Launch Activity"

- "Set a security alarm for 6 AM tomorrow"

- "Call [anyone]"

- "Send a note to [anyone]"

- "Play the Beatles"

- "Remind me to [do something] at [time] or on [day]"

- "Collection a 10-minute timer"

- "Get traveling directions to the closest gas train station"

- "What's the end on the [any buck amount] expenses?"

- And several other commands, including commands for specific applications such as "Call Phil on Skype"

How to begin a good work out With Apple Watch

Most of us leap in to the world of smartwatches for the fitness side rather than answering that text or telephone call without getting into our pocket for our telephone. Apple Watch has two primary exercise apps: the experience app, which songs normal activity on a regular basis, and the Workout app, that allows you to monitor specific workouts.

The Activity application is fantastic. You can transform your goal by utilizing a Pressure Touch press, and you may get more descriptive reviews including historical information by releasing the activity application on your iPhone. However, the exercise goal within the experience app is a simple exercise monitor that simply paths your active amount of time in bands of 30 mins without way to customize it.

That is where the Apple Watch's Workout application makes the picture. Starting a good work out is really as easy as 1-2-3:

- **Start the Workout app.** This is actually the green application with the physique running.

- **Pick from the set of workouts.** There is certainly everything from operating to going swimming to bicycling to rowing or even yoga exercise. Unless you see your exercise on the list, simply choose Other.

- **Touch the workout.** The Apple Watch will count number down from three and then start monitoring your activity. If you are done, swipe from left-to-right on the display screen and choose End. You can even faucet Pause to have a brief break or Drinking water Lock if your exercise is in the pool.

Exercises are tracked through the experience application

on your iPhone in the Exercises tab. You will see a written report of a person exercise by tapping it in the list. The statement will include calorie consumption burnt, total time and average heartrate. It will record the elements during the workout, and if you possess an Apple Watch with GPS navigation, where you are and route will be documented on the map.

How exactly to Customize Apple Watch Through Settings

The Apple Watch has a Settings application on the watch itself and a couple of configurations access through the Watch application on the iPhone. Regrettably, the majority of these configurations aren't simply duplicates. While there are many configurations available in both places, additionally there is specific customization only available through the Watch application or on the watch itself.

- The Apple Watch's Settings application stocks the same "gears turning" icon as the Settings application on the iPhone. It offers the capability to arranged the enough time forward for individuals who like their watch to perform faster than the real time, start or off configurations like Bluetooth or Aircraft mode, adjust the appearance and feel of the watch, and customize general configurations like convenience and Siri.

- The Watch application on the iPhone is the greater comprehensive of both. You can not only find lots of the same configurations within the watch's Settings app, you can also change your application layout, change the dock, set up Emergency SOS, customize Personal privacy configurations and fine-tune person apps.

CHAPTER 2

How To Repair Apple Watch: All You Need To Know

Despite being truly a fashionable timepiece, the Apple Watch is also a sophisticated little bit of technology and, unfortunately, could find itself faltering or facing issues as any other computerized device would. This guide identifies a few of the most typical Apple Watch issues and ways to see needs to repair them.

The sources of Apple Watch Issues

Your Apple Watch is a completely functioning small computer that lives on your wrist, so issues are probably not traced back again to the same cause. An entire processing solution means that we now have various different problems and solutions available depending on precisely what is happening with your Watch.

How To Fix Connection Problems With Apple Watch

Occasionally, you might find that your Watch won't connect to your iPhone, a known Wi-Fi network, or an LTE connection. Follow these steps to really get your Apple Watch back communication with the world.

- Change Bluetooth Off: In case your iPhone watching are experiencing trouble communicating, you should start by turning off the Bluetooth function on each device, then turning it back to reestablish an association.

  o iPhone: Settings > Bluetooth > Toggle Off/On

  o Apple Watch: Swipe Up > Bluetooth Icon > Toggle Off/On

- Restart Your Devices: If simply deactivating your Bluetooth for an instant doesn't fix the communication concern, restart both your iPhone and Apple Watch so that they can reestablish a standard connection.

- Bring back an LTE Connection: In case your Apple Watch normally connects to the internet with a cellular connection, but has ceased to take action, start by either toggling Aircraft Setting on and then off, or restart your device completely.

  o Apple Watch: Swipe Up > Aircraft Setting > Toggle Off/On

- Connecting to Wi-Fi Systems: In case your iPhone is not around, your Apple Watch can try to hook up to a known Wi-Fi network for access to the internet. In case your Watch is not linking, make sure that your iPhone uses the network and has already established an opportunity to share the info with your Watch.

- Improper Pairing: In the event that you recently restored your iPhone or purchased a fresh device, your Apple Watch might not be properly setup with your telephone. It is possible to set an Apple Watch with an iPhone for greater detail.

How To Fix Electric Battery Problems With Apple Watch

Is your Apple Watch draining its battery rapidly? Here are some suggestions you might desire to view to really get your device's electric battery in order without hassle.

- Enable Energy Saving Mode: If you are looking to extend your Watch's electric battery life, easy and simple option is to allow Power Saving Setting in the Apple Watch app; this will disable the heartrate sensor from activating during walking and exercises. The feature can make you calorie burn off less accurate, but will preserve your electric battery life.

- o Apple Watch: Apple Watch application > Workout > Energy Saving Mode

- Optimize Your Apple Watch: If Energy Saving Setting isn't doing enough, you can further lessen your watch's battery consumption by restricting notifications that light the display and shutting off Wi-Fi on your Apple Watch.

- o Apple Watch: Swipe Up > Wi-Fi Icon > Toggle Off

- Give it a Reboot: Sometimes everything is really as simple as a reboot. In case your Apple Watch appears to be draining electric battery life like there is absolutely no tomorrow, simply turn the watch off then back again on again may be helpful

- do this by keeping down the Watch's part button until Power Off function shows.

- Get the Watch Charging Again: In case your Apple Watch battery has ceased to charge, it might be broken. We recommend phoning Apple for support or scheduling a scheduled appointment with an Apple Store Genius Pub.

How Exactly To Fix Physical Problems With Apple Watch

None of the Apple Watch's hardware is serviceable by users at home, and can typically need a Genius Club visit or support call to get fixed; however, here are some recommendations for common issues.

- Get the Digital Crown Working Smoothly: Apple's Digital Crown has been recognized to have issues where it could become difficult to carefully turn if dirty. To find solution the situation, remove your Apple Watch rings, then rinse these devices with tepid to warm water, while revolving the Digital Crown for approximately 30 seconds.

- Repairing Broken Displays: Unfortunately, if your Apple Watch's display is becoming damaged, it must be repaired by a certified Apple repair service. We recommend taking the watch to your neighborhood Apple Store for a Genius Pub appointment.

- Have Your Heartrate Sensed: May be the Apple Watch not picking right up your heartrate? Don't be concerned, you remain alive! By making sure your Apple Watch is guaranteed firmly enough against your skin layer, as a baggy watch won't monitor anything. Additionally, if you have dark colored tattoos on your wrist, your watch may not track the heartrate as it struggles to sense your vein.

The Final Resort for Software Problems

In case your Apple Watch is experiencing a variety of software issues, or just one which you can't overcome. Apple Support may advise that you reset your Watch.

CHAPTER 3

New Apple Watch Discussions: Some Tips About What To Expect

Just a couple years following its debut, the Apple Watch is the most fashionable and, possibly the hottest, smartwatch on the marketplace. That's because of its mixture of style, features, and integration with the iPhone.

Using the second-generation Apple Watch Series 2 having been on the marketplace some time, attention is embracing what comes next for the Watch.

You will find major new features coming to the Apple Watch; however, the rumor mill is split on exactly when they'll debut. Some expect that the Apple Watch Series 3 will get to 2018 packing all types of futuristic tech.

Alternatively, some observers say that the Series 3 is to arrive 2017 and can sport only a few small improvements, with the 2018 Series 4 providing the major increases.

Due to that uncertainty, the primary part of the article addresses the rumored changes to the Apple Watch that appear most likely.

Things to Expect from The Apple Watch Series 3:

- All features within the Series 2 model

- Micro-LED Screen

- Faster processor

- Smaller and thinner

- Somewhat improved electric battery life

- Sleep tracking

- Smart watch rings

More Info On The Apple Watch 3 Gossips

Following the original Apple Watch, Apple introduced the Apple Watch Series 1 and Series 2. The Series 1 really was just a genuine Apple Watch with a much-improved processor chip and a lower price. The Series 2 added a much better display, the faster processor chip, and serious waterproofing. We completely expect another watch to keep those features and also to continue the naming custom and become called the Series 3.

Display: Brighter and More Efficient

Expect the next-generation Apple Watch to employ a micro-LED display screen. This technology is a much better version of the OLED display in today's models and really should provide a brighter image and require less electric battery life. A longer-lasting electric battery is always best for a wearable, and a brighter display is a large help with all the watch in sunshine.

Better Brains: Faster Processor chip

Exactly like every new iPhone is made around a fresh processor chip, each new version of the Apple Watch gets a smarter brain. Be prepared to start to see the Apple Watch Series 3 sporting an Apple S3 chip. The leap from the S1P in the first-generation Apple Watch to the S2 in the Series 2 shipped an apparent improvement in velocity and power. Don't expect the same benefits these times, but even a little speed increase never hurts.

New Design: Smaller, Leaner Body

As the Apple Watch Series 2 was heavier than the initial Apple Watch, it was a rare instance of Apple being un-Apple-like. To become clear, we're discussing three to four 4 grams here (a gram is approximately the weight of a typical paperclip), so it is doubtful many people even experienced a notable difference. Expect those grams to vanish with the Apple Watch Series 3. Although it is probably not leaner or lighter than the initial model, we'd wager that the Series 3 will tilt the scales significantly less than the Series 2.

Electric Battery Life: Improved, But Just How Much?

Battery pack life was a significant part of improvement for the Series 2 set alongside the original Apple Watch. The electric battery went from requiring a charge every day to requiring power nearer to almost every other day. That might not appear to be much, but that's in regards to a 100% improvement. Electric battery life is a significant asset for Apple devices, so we ought to expect the Series 3 to go longer than the Series 2. Just how much longer is a huge question, though. Another 100% improvement in electric battery life seems most unlikely.

New Features: Rest Monitoring and Smart Rings That Deliver More

The Apple Watch is ideal for fitness tracking-steps,

calories, heartrate, etc.-but modern exercise science demonstrates getting good sleep can be essential for you to get good exercise. Apple appeared to trust this view when it bought the sleep-tracking application Beddit. Be prepared to see Beddit, or at least its features, dealing with the Series 3 to help you realize whether you are getting good rest.

There were plentiful rumors that future Apple Watch models will have bands that do more than contain the watch on your wrist. These "smart rings" would actually deliver some type of features. A number of the popular gossips include a music group with an electric battery in it for extra life, moving the haptic engine (the hardware which makes the Watch vibrate) in to the music group to help make the watch itself smaller, or perhaps a music group that can screen things such as the time.

Health features that are notably missing, like the blood sugar monitor mentioned below, can also be delivered through a good band. This may easily have been categorized in the improbable features below, but there is a chance at least some version of the features will arrive with the Series 3.

Very Cool-But Unlikely-Features

These features are rumored to be contained in future versions of the Apple Watch, but we think they're improbable showing up in the Series 3:

- FaceTime-Being in a position to make telephone and video phone calls from your Watch would make it feel just like the near future is currently, but it could need a built-in camera. That might be difficult for such a little device, and if it only worked well over Wi-Fi, is that a lot of an improvement more than a telephone, tablet, or Mac pc?

- 4G LTE-An Apple Watch that can place calls more

than a 4G LTE network is a dream. It'll probably stay a desire until Apple can find out ways to get a much longer-lasting electric battery in to the Watch, though.

- Blood Sugar Monitoring-Apple is reportedly focusing on features that could check bloodstream sugars level through your skin, without needles or bloodstream. This might make the Apple Watch a must-have device for diabetics. With considerable screening and FDA approvals essential for this feature, the jury has gone out whether we'll view it anytime soon.

CHAPTER 4

The 9 Best Apple Watch Accessories of 2019

The Rundown

Best Overall: Apple Air Pods at Amazon, "The bond never drops and it is among the best we've experienced in true Wi-Fi earphones."

Best Budget: LK Display screen Protector at Amazon, "They have hydrophobic and oleophobic clear layers, which protects the cup against from fingerprints."

Best Charging Dock: Belkin Watch Valet Charge Dock for Apple Watch at Amazon, "Comes with an armrest that keeps the watch at a position for optimal looking at, along with a magnetic charger."

Best All-in-one Charging Dock: *Kehangda* 3 in 1 Charging Stand at Amazon, "This Amazon favorite is affordable at under $20 but nonetheless has a sleek design and durable build."

Best Armband: 12 South Armband for 42mm Apple Watch at Amazon, "Because of tighter and more constant pores and skin contact, the heartrate monitor could work more accurately."

Best Battery Power: 700mAh Smart Keychain Power Lender at Amazon, "Having a 700mAh electric battery, it juices up your Watch to completely in around 45 minutes."

Best Watch Case: Spigen Rugged Armor Apple Watch Case at Amazon, "This Apple Watch case sits around these devices to safeguard it against bumps and scrapes."

Best for Travelers: 12 South Time Porter for Apple Watch at Amazon, "This 12 South Time Porter is the travel friend you'll want."

Best for Sports athletes: Polar H10 Heartrate Monitor at Amazon, "This heartrate monitor from Polar is flawlessly appropriate for your Apple Watch."

The Apple Watch puts all the capability of an iPhone directly on your wrist, but if you would like to hear music or make calls, you'll need a set of compatible headphones. Our favorites will be the Apple Air Pods, which arranged the typical for true cellular earphones. After a breezy preliminary set up, these earphones automatically hook up to your device (both iOS and Google android) when you put them in your ears. The bond never drops and it is among the best we've experienced in true cellular earphones, which, regrettably, isn't the situation for all those cellular headphones.

Want to pause your music or answer phone calls? The

settings are right close at hand, actually: To activate Siri, just say "Hey, Siri" or dual touch on the remaining earbud; to miss tracks, double faucet on the right earbud. So, when you take one earbud out, they easily pause the audio. There are many different ways the Apple Watch can enhance productivity.

The most recent model looks almost identical to the prior ones - white plastic with an equally sleek charging case - precisely what you'd expect from Cupertino. The main one noticeable change is the move of the LED charging light in the case to the exterior - where it ought to be, inside our opinion. The light indicators red when they may be charging and green when completely charged. Apple statements the electric battery life continues about five hours about the same charge, however in fact, they come in nearer to four hours plus some change. That's much less impressive as various other cellular earphones on the marketplace but it's still about 20 percent much longer than the prior version of Apple's Air Pods. The most known update? The situation is now able to charge wirelessly, similar to the Apple Watch. (A cheaper model is available with no cellular charging case.)

The Apple Watch feels durable, especially set alongside the more delicate iPhones. Even though the stunning Retina screen is constructed of Ion-X strengthened cup, it's still not completely shatterproof. To become on the safe part, slap on the display screen protector that doesn't prevent efficiency. This LK display protector is both budget-friendly and touch-sensitive, therefore the display still shows up bright and amazing.

Application is simple via wet set up and the initial adhesive can be washed, reused and reapplied. The display screen protector is merely 18mm thick therefore the display retains its response sensitivity without stickiness. They have hydrophobic and oleophobic clear layers, which protects the cup protects against everything perspiration and essential oil residue from fingerprints, as well as more intense scuff marks. The protector works with Series 1, 2, 3 and 4, and the pack includes six display protectors.

By the end of your day, when you remove your watch, you'll need an equally elegant stand to put it on. Belkin, a brand name that has been known because of its smooth and functional technology accessories, makes one of well-known charging docks, appropriate for all available Apple Watches. The refined white base suits properly with Apple's visual and it is weighted such that it doesn't easily suggestion over. They have a chromium armrest that keeps that watch at a position for optimal looking at, along with a built-in magnetic charger that starts charging instantly. There's also a wrist music group support that you can slip the wristband around to keep up its shape. The bottom is tethered to a four-foot USB-A wire (included) and that means you can easily place it on the bedside desk or table to charge.

If you're like the majority of Apple Watch owners, you almost certainly likewise have an iPhone and Air Pods. If so, you'll want a dock that charges all of your devices concurrently. This Amazon favorite is affordable at under $20 but nonetheless has a smooth design and durable build. It's appropriate for all available types of the Apple Watch, Air Pods and iPhone 6 and later.

The 3-in-1 base is constructed of premium silicone material with a soft finish to ensure your devices don't get scratched. Set up is fairly easy, needing you to thread the charging cables from the device. Because they use the initial cables, charging velocity is simply as fast as a standard wall structure charger would be. All devices are obviously displayed which means you can easily see necessary notifications and it even accommodates devices with solid instances. (An Air Pod travel case is roofed as well.)

The wonder of the Apple Watch is it puts the energy of your iPhone right around your wrist, but sometimes certain sports gear (boxing gloves, for instance) prohibits you from wrist placement. In those situations, this Action Sleeve straps around your top arm, moving it out of harm's way however, not out of reach. Simply take your Look out of its wrist music group and pop it in to the armband; the display screen, crown, and button stay fully accessible. Even better, because of tighter and more constant epidermis contact, the heartrate monitor could work more accurately. The armband, available in red or dark, works with all Apple Watch models and it is suitable for hands up to 13 ins in circumference.

Relating to Apple, the Apple Watch's battery is maintained about 18 hours, predicated on 90-time bank checks, 90 notifications, 45 minutes of application use and 60 minutes of music playtime via Bluetooth. But if you're like the majority of people, you almost certainly check your watch a lot more than that. Which makes this keychain battery power even more useful, It could clip on your key band or back pack and comes with an integrated MFI-certified magnetic charging component. Using a 700mAh electric battery, it juices up your Watch to completely in around 45 minutes and four LED indication lights to transmission the position of charging. It protects your Watch from over-current, over-charging and over-heating and works with all models, including Apple Watch Sport, Apple Watch Nike+, Apple Watch Hermès, and Apple Watch Release. The keychain itself charges backup via USB.

Instead of a display protector, this Apple Watch case sits around these devices to safeguard it against bumps and scrapes. It's created from durable TPU materials that is durable yet doesn't add too much mass. The situation is elevated 1.2mm to safeguard the display, so while a display screen protector is neither necessary nor included, you can always apply someone to be extra safe. In addition, it has an aluminum button for solid opinions and a cutout on the trunk for hassle-free charging. Appropriate for the 42mm Watch (Series 1, 2 and 3), we recommend purchasing the smaller, 38mm display screen protector if you opt to add one, normally, the display protector might peel from the lime slightly.

If you're on the highway often, this Twelve Southern Time Porter is the travel companion you'll want. It works as both an organizer and a charger, keeping your Apple Watch necessities like charging cables, wrist rings, and travel adapters. The silicone-lined interior of the situation has spools and that means you can summary your unruly cables and a portal retains the charging disc flush with the external surface of Time Porter which means you can place your Watch over the leather case for charging. In the event that you store a radio battery power inside, you can change your Time Porter into a radio charging station, ideal for camping and alternative activities where you don't have a wall structure outlet handy.

As the Apple Watch comes with an integrated heartrate monitor, it isn't incredibly accurate. Sportsmen know that the ultimate way to get a heartrate reading has been an ardent heartrate monitor, which one from Polar is flawlessly appropriate for your Apple Watch. They have built-in memory space that can store a complete training session and its own battery has approximately 400 hours of functional time. The H10 pairs easily with both Google android and iOS devices, together with your Apple Watch, but if you set it with a GoPro Hero, you can overlay your heartrate data onto the documented video. On the other hand, you can use smart training when you set it with the Polar Defeat mobile application to get unique responses. The strap is smooth and comfortable, available in sizes XS to XXXL and four colors: dark, grey, orange and turquoise.

CHAPTER 5

15 Best Weight Reduction Apps for Apple Watch In 2019

Have you started a weight loss trip? If so, you might have committed to an Apple Watch, the perfect partner for achieving weight reduction and workout goals. Monitor your calorie consumption, weight, practices and more by using this assortment of Apple Watch weight reduction apps.

Best for Keeping track of Basic Nourishment Facts:
Food visor - Calorie Counter

Food visor is the best calorie counter-top and nutrition truth finder for every meal imaginable. Using the in-app features, you need to a photo making use of your iPhone of your dish to see nourishment facts. The application tells you if your food is balanced.

You can even log your steps and exercise to observe how many calories you've burned in comparison to your logged meals. Regrettably, you can't add foods straight from your Watch, nevertheless, you can see your present calorie position from your wrist.

Although the application is absolve to download, you can buy Food visor High quality for usage of recipes, weight loss programs and a live speak to a nutritionist. Programs range between $9.99 per month to $59.88 per 12 months.

Best GPS Navigation Working Tracker: Run keeper - GPS navigation Running Tracker

Rated as among the best GPS operating trackers in the App Store, run keeper by ASICS gives you to monitor your workouts, established your own goals, produce a customized plan, and more, all in a single app.

What units Run keeper in addition to the remaining running applications is the capability to monitor your stats on your Apple Watch without your iPhone. In-app issues and exercise rewards keep you motivated on your bodyweight loss fitness trip. Plus, there's a lot of competition training programs for those attempting to enjoy their first marathon.

Run keeper is absolve to download but offers reduced version which include side-by-side workout comparisons, weather data and more. Prices range between $9.99 per month to $39.99 per year.

Best for Fun Exercises: Zombies, Run!

If you want some motivation to reduce those extra few pounds, zombies might do just fine. Zombies, Run is a great, story-based workout monitoring application that immerses you in a zombie apocalypse. Every run you take becomes an objective of escape.

The application contains 200+ missions, something new for each workout. As you run or walk, you'll pay attention as you're instructed on how to proceed next. You'll gather materials to help you survive as you pay attention to your own music. And yes, the application works likewise on a treadmill machine as it can around the recreation area.

Zombies, Run is absolve to download, but takes a pro membership to unlock all storylines and features, like unlimited play and intensive training. Prices range between $5.99 to $34.99.

Best for Monitoring Your Weight Reduction Success: MyFitnessPal

Weight reduction is an activity that will often take years to perform. You will need a solid app that will help you monitor your improvement from day one. MyFitnessPal is an entire weight loss monitoring application that showcases your bodyweight over time plus your daily diet intake, exercise and more.

The nutrition data source is huge and addresses an array of brands, restaurants and more. Making use of your Apple Watch, you can quick add your drinking water intake plus your calories, causing this to be app stick out from other calorie keeping track of apps upon this list.

MyFitnessPal is absolve to download and use but offers reduced version to offer usage of the Nutrient Dashboard, Calorie Goals by Food, the capability to quick add your carbs, protein, and body fat as well as much other features. Programs range between $9.99 to $49.99.

Best for Tracking Your Hydration: My Drinking water Balance

My Drinking water Balance can help you monitor your drinking water intake, which is crucial to any weight reduction goal. The application also gives you to monitor other drinks such as tea and carbonated drinks. As you monitor your consumption, the application creates charts that you should see your improvement.

Gleam drinking water requirement calculator to help you regulate how much drinking water you need per day. Of course, you need to consider your way of life, activity level, and weight reduction goals for a particular requirement.

My Drinking water Balance is simple to use on the Apple Watch, providing you the option to include entries right from your wrist. My Drinking water Balance is absolve to use but takes a high quality membership to unlock all drink options. Prices range between $4.99 per month to $29.99 a year.

Best for Monitoring Your Macros: Life sum Diet & Macro Tracker

If you want to monitor your macros at length, Life sum is

a superb addition to your Apple Watch. From your own iPhone, you can enter your daily water and food consumption to see your present dietary stats. Then, view your improvement during the day on your iPhone.

Life sum offers you the choice to see healthy quality recipes in the app, depending on your daily diet. You are able to choose from diets such as keto, fasting, Mediterranean, and more. Gleam basic food prep option with recommendations for those looking for the "down for you" method of a diet program.

Life sum is absolve to download and use but takes a superior subscription for dishes, specialized diets, and other features. Prices range between $21.99 for 90 days to $44.99 for a year.

Best For Training Fast: Seven - 7 Minute Workout

The seven-minute workout has been hailed as a terrific way to enter a high-intensity workout in a brief timeframe, boosting weight loss efforts. Seven can be an Apple Watch application that provides you usage of a library of seven-minute exercises to suit your weight reduction goals.

As you work out, your Apple Watch will display illustrations showing you how to proceed. You can even pause or end your workout from your Watch. You are able to choose your targets such as get exercise or lose weight to tailor your workout routines to your targets. Seven will also remind you if it is time for you to work out every day.

Seven includes several basic workouts to truly get you started. To gain access to all exercises available and over 200 exercises, you will need to buy the 7 Golf club premium regular membership. Prices range between $9.99 per month to $79.99 a year.

Best for Discovering Healthy Recipes: Yummy

Recipes

Grocery List

Probably one of the most difficult elements of weight reduction is wanting to find healthy formulas that flavor good. Yummy requires the guesswork from it all by recommending recipes predicated on your favorite food, allergies, and dislikes. Plus, you can save all your favorites inside the application and view them on your Apple Watch.

You can produce a shopping list for every formula that populates on your Apple Watch out for easy shopping. Although you must by hand delete items from the list, you can checkmark them on your Watch. The Apple Watch tone of voice search option also can help you find meals hands-free.

Yummy is totally absolve to download and use. All features are for sale to use as there is no premium version.

Best for Meal Prepping: Meal PrepPro Meal Prep Planner

Food prepping makes sticking with a fresh plan simple. Meal PrepPro is an entire meal prepping application that creates an idea for you. Unless you like what they choose, you can get into your iPhone and change meals around. You can even track your drinking water intake plus your macros and calorie consumption inside the app.

Your Apple Watch updates with your improvement each day. You can even check your daily foods from your list from your Watch. There are numerous quality recipes available, but most require some cooking food skill to perform.

Meal PrepPro is absolve to download for a 7-day trial. From then on, you'll need to buy a premium membership. Prices range between $5.99 per month to $47.99 a year.

Best Preinstalled Activity Tracker: Activity

The Apple Watch includes the Activity application that offers a user-friendly user interface and a simple summary of your daily activity. You are able to receive notifications if it is time so that you can move, perfect for individuals who work in offices or in sedentary positions.

The Activity application shows just how many calories you've burnt per day, as well as just how many minutes of exercise you've completed. Goals are arranged depending on your life style and habits.

Apple's Activity application is absolve to download and use both on the iPhone and the Apple Watch.

Best for Monitoring Your Calorie consumption: Lose It! Calorie Counter

Although many of the apps provide a calorie counter, it might be easier to come with an app designed for entering your calories every day. Lose It really is an entire calorie counter which allows you to monitor your daily intake of calorie consumption, macros, protein and more.

The recipe data source is large and also you have the choice to scan barcodes to find your exact nutritional information for most different brands. Nutritional information that is proven by the Lose It team has a green checkmark for easy precision.

Lose It really is absolve to download and use but offers reduced membership for features such as understanding which foods are sabotaging your bodyweight reduction and more. Prices range between $4.99 per month to $39.99 a year.

Best for Sound Workout routines: Aaptiv Sound Fitness

Have you got an individual trainer for your bodyweight reduction goals? Or, do you like having audio training for your workout routines? Aaptiv is a superb audio workout application which includes many unique exercises that you can choose from. Plus, you get access to your favorite workout routines on your Apple Watch.

To begin with, you find a good work out you intend to use and download it. You'll then pay attention as the trainer tells you how to proceed next. Some goes are problematic for beginners without prior knowledge. But just a little practice makes perfect.

To access the majority of the exercises, you will need to buy an Aaptiv subscription. Prices range between $14.99 to $99.99 for unlimited on-demand classes.

Best App for Keto: Carb Manager

For those on the weight loss journey with keto, you will need an app that matters your daily carbohydrates. Carb Supervisor does that as well as monitoring your online carbs, total carbs, and diabetes carbs. The application also provides you usage of a large number of keto-friendly dishes for easy food planning.

You can include new recipes predicated on your own cooking food to make sure you don't miss a carb. Health monitoring is available and that means you can monitor your weight reduction improvement. Although there's a little of the learning curve to obtain it right, this application is ideal for monitoring keto success.

Carb Supervisor is absolve to download but takes a high quality membership to unlock all formulas, health monitoring and more. Prices range between $8.49 monthly to $39.99 per year.

Best for Monitoring Your Weight Reduction Practices: Done

Part of an effective weight loss trip is developing new behaviors such as taking in more drinking water or steering clear of sugary beverages. The Done habit tracker will help you build or stop practices depending on your targets. Done is user friendly and provides you the capability to complete goals making use of your Apple Watch.

In the app, you can include up to three unique habits or goals using the free version (unlimited with an upgrade). You are able to established how you want your behaviors to look, take down notes about them, add motivational estimates and more.

Done is absolve to download and use. To unlock unlimited habit and goal monitoring, you may need a high-quality subscription. The purchase price is $6.99 for a one-time upgrade.

Best for Intermittent Fasting: No Fasting Tracker

For all those using intermittent fasting within their weight loss program, zero is the perfect companion. Pick from popular fasts such as 16:8 or Circadian Tempo, or create your own fast using the app.

After your fast, you can rate how you feel it went and add any notes you intend to add. You will also earn badges by completing milestones and receive education on protocols for the safest fasting methods. You can begin and stop an easy easily making use of your Apple Watch.

Zero is absolve to download and use. You will have to create a merchant account prior to having the ability to use the app.

CHAPTER 6

The 8 Best Apple Watch Stands of 2019

Best Overall: Belkin Valet Charge Dock Stand at Amazon

"A sensational metallic chrome end allows the watch to be propped at an optimal looking at position while being charged."

Best for Charging: Apple Watch Magnetic Charging Dock at Best Buy

"Ridiculously simple…let us charge the watch either in a set position or on its part."

Best With Telephone/Tablet Support: Mercase Apple Watch Stand at Amazon

"Appropriate for all Apple Watch models (Series 1 to 4), as well as nearly all smartphones and tablets."

Best With Additional USB Charging Slot: Mangotek Charging Stand at Amazon

"May be used to charge from smartphones to power banking institutions, utilizing a simple USB wire."

Best Splurge: Belkin Power House Dock at Amazon

"The Lightning slot extending from its foundation, which enables you to charge your iPhone simply by putting it on the stand."

Best Budget: Spigen S350 at Amazon

"Compact and light-weight, it features an open up dock design."

Best Design: Elago W3 at Amazon

"Modeled after Apple's original Macintosh 128K pc, which arrived in 1984."

Best For In-Car Usage: Elago W Stand at Amazon

"Design enables you to keep carefully the stand in your car's glass holder, which makes it a cakewalk to charge your Apple Watch on the road."

With regards to accessories for modern electronic devices, Belkin is a name that you can always trust. Therefore, the Valet Charge Dock Stand is the best Apple Watch stand you're heading to find.

Belkin Valet Charge Dock Stand has a design that's as high quality as it's functional. As the name suggests, this stand also enables you to charge the Apple Watch. It includes a built-in magnetic charging component, integrated into an increased armrest. Having a sensational metallic chrome surface finish, the armrest allows the watch to be propped at an ideal viewing position while being billed. The included music group support connection neatly clips to the charger, which makes it easy to keep versatile watch rings such as metal mesh and hyperlink bracelets supported. The complete armrest set up is affixed to a white high-polished bottom, which is weighted for improved stability. The bottom also includes a four-foot long tethered USB Type-A wire you can use to power the stand utilizing a wall structure adapter. Belkin's Valet Charge Dock Stand works with all Apple Watch (up to Series 3) models, including Sport and Release.

If you're searching for a simple Apple Watch stand that can also charge the wearable, you don't even need to work with third-party solutions. Just get the Magnetic Charging Dock, created by non-e apart from Apple.

Ridiculously straightforward to use, Apple Watch Magnetic Charging Dock enables you to charge the watch either in a set position (with the band undone) or on its side. For docking, all you need to do is lift the magnetic charging component from the guts of the stand

and prop the watch against it. When docked on its aspect, Apple Watch automatically switches into the "Nightstand" setting, letting you utilize it as a bedside noisy alarm. The dock uses the same inductive charging connection that is included with Apple Watch. It connects with a Lightning to USB wire and uses Apple's 5W USB power adapter (sold individually). Also, since it's created by Apple, compatibility isn't a concern. Apple Watch Magnetic Charging Dock may charge both 38mm and 42mm sizes and works with all Apple Watch models (Series 1 to 4). It's supported with an one-year limited warranty.

Stylish and flexible, Mercase's Apple Watch Stand enables you to prop up your smartwatch easily. However, what truly makes this stand amazing is that as well as the watch, additionally, it may keep your smartphone or tablet.

Mercase Apple Watch Stand features an increased system

for docking the watch at an optimal position. It can keep Apple Watch's charging puck as well, allowing the wearable to be utilized as a noisy alarm in "Nightstand" setting. The system is attached with the bottom at the trunk, with the support -panel for the smartphone/tablet propped up (at a 120-level angle) in leading. It can contain the smartphone even though the latter is within a solid case. The complete stand is made of aluminum, with Apple Watch dock using a coating of scratch-free TPU over it. The support panel has a coating of scratch-resistant silicone, while plastic feet at the bottom of the stand provide improved stability and hold. Mercase Apple Watch Stand works with all Apple Watch models (Series 1 to 4), as well as nearly all smartphones and tablets. It's also supported by an eternity warranty.

You'll find so many Apple Watch stands available out there that enable you to charge the smartwatch, which is fantastic. But, imagine if you could utilize someone to juice up your other devices, Say hello to Mangotek Charging Stand.

Even while a standalone Apple Watch charger, Mangotek's stand works quite nicely. It possesses a raised armrest having a built-in magnetic charging component (with support for "Nightstand" setting), which springs into action as soon as you place the smartwatch onto it. The armrest is affixed to a soft-finish foundation that's both durable and superior looking. However, the best feature of Mangotek Charging Stand is an ardent USB Type-A interface, on the part of the bottom. Using a power result of 2.1A, it could be used to charge from smartphones to power banking institutions, utilizing a simple USB wire. These devices being billed can be positioned on the stand's bottom itself, therefore the entire arrangement remains clutter-free. Mangotek Charging Stand works with most Apple Watch models (up to Series 3), and it is driven by 5V/3A adapter. It's supported with one-year warranty.

When you have an Apple Watch, it's basically certain that you utilize an iPhone as well. Wouldn't it be great if you could charge both simply by placing them collectively on the stand? Enter Belkin Power House Dock.

Despite the fact that it's only a penny shy of the Benjamin, the Power House Dock is obviously worth the purchase price. It includes an elevated docking arm that's flawlessly angled to carry Apple Watch. The arm, which is prolonged towards right, includes a magnetic charging module for the smartwatch. Having said that, the best feature of Belkin Power House Dock is the Lightning slot increasing from its foundation, which enables you to charge your iPhone simply by putting it on the stand. Not just that, you can easily adjust the elevation of the Lightning interface using the built-in "Versa Case" dial, allowing the iPhone(s) to be billed with the majority of the protective instances. The stand has a mixed result of

3.4A (1A for Apple Watch and 2.4A for iPhone) and includes a 1.2m long power wire. Belkin Power House Dock comes in two colors - dark and white.

Nice Apple Watch stands using their laundry set of features are indeed great, but they're hardly ever affordable. If you're on a budget and want something simpler, you might have a look at Spigen S350.

Compact and light-weight, the S350 gets the same quality that Spigen's smartphone instances are recognized for. It features an open up dock design, that allows it to be easily used in combination with Apple Watch's bundled magnetic charging puck. Completely appropriate for the wearable's "Nightstand" setting, it may charge Apple Watch whether or not its strap is shut or open up. Spigen S350 is manufactured out of durable TPU materials and includes a slip-resistant "Nanotac" bottom. There's also an adhesive silicon pad, which ensures better compatibility with the 38mm model. The stand works similarly well with all Apple Watch models, from Series 1 to Series 4. It's available in a number of colors - white, midnight blue, red sand, dark, and volt dark.

There's something unique about the designs of yesteryears' devices, which continue being endearing right now. Love everything old and want to provide your modern Apple Watch a vintage touch? Get the Elago W3.

Elago W3 isn't just the best-designed Apple Watch stick out there, it's also the most adorable. It's modeled after Apple's original Macintosh 128K pc, which arrived in 1984. The stand is manufactured out of high-quality silicon that's both versatile and scratch-resistant. A near-perfect imitation of the Macintosh, it even includes a floppy drive slot machine. To use the W3, all you need to do is dock your Apple Watch onto it. The wearable's screen lines up properly with the stand's front side cut-out, offering the impression of a vintage CRT display. The stand works great with Apple Watch's bundled magnetic charging puck and includes an opening at the trunk for proper wire management. Appropriate for "Nightstand" setting, Elago W3 comes in two colors - traditional white and dark.

Most watch stands are designed to be utilized in a set location (e.g. bedside), and that's how it preferably should be. However, there could be times when you will need to juice up your Apple Watch while you're moving (e.g. in an automobile). For all those times, Elago's W Stand will last just fine.

Having reduced aluminum construction, Elago W Stand is among the best accessories you can get for Apple Watch. Its top and bottom level panels are constructed of silicon to avoid any harm to the wearable, as well as the top that the stand is continued. The cylindrical design produces great wire management, allowing even the longest wire to be stowed away sans any issues. But even moreover, that design enables you to keep carefully the stand in your car's glass holder, which makes it a cakewalk to charge your Apple Watch on the road. Appropriate for all Apple Watch models (Series 1 to 4), Elago W Stand helps "Nightstand" setting. You get five colors to choose from - dark, silver, champagne platinum, dark grey, and rose yellow metal.

Acknowledgments

The Glory of this book success goes to God Almighty and my beautiful Family, Fans, Readers & well-wishers, Customers and Friends for their endless support and encouragements.

CPSIA information can be obtained
at www.ICGtesting.com
Printed in the USA
BVHW040450280321
603587BV00009B/2858